1

The Constitution of
The State of New Hampshire:
A Quick Reference Guide

Bootblack Budget Books
Copyright 2018 ©
ISBN-13: 978-1717052841
ISBN-10: 1717052843

Contents:

PART FIRST- BILL OF RIGHTS – Page 13

Article 1. Equality of Men; Origin and Object of Government

Article 2. Natural Rights

Article 2-A. The Bearing of Arms

Article 3. Society, it's Organization and Purposes

Article 4. Rights of Conscience Unalienable

Article 5. Religious Freedom Recognized

Article 6. Morality and Piety

Article 7. State Sovereignty

Article 8. Accountability of Magistrates and Officers; Public's Right to Know

Article 9. No Hereditary Office Or Place

Article 10. Right of Revolution

Article 11. Elections and Elective Franchises

Article 12. Protection and Taxation Reciprocal

Article 12-A. Power To Take Property Limited

Article 13. Conscientious Objectors not Compelled to Bear Arms

Article 14. Legal Remedies to be Free, Complete, and Prompt

Article 15. Right of Accused

Article 16. Former Jeopardy; Jury Trial in Capital Cases

Article 17. Venue of Criminal Prosecution

Article 18. Penalties to be Proportioned to Offenses; True Design of Punishment

Article 19. Searches and Seizures Regulated

Article 20. Jury Trial in Civil Causes

Article 21. Jurors; Compensation

Article 22. Free Speech; Liberty of The Press

Article 23. Retrospective Laws Prohibited

Article 24. Militia

Article 25. Standing Armies

Article 26. Military, Subject to Civil Power

Article 27. Quartering of Soldiers

Article 28. Taxes, by Whom Levied

Article 28-A. Mandated Programs

Article 29. Suspension of Laws by Legislature Only

Article 30. Freedom of Speech

Article 31. Meetings of Legislature, For What Purposes

Article 32. Rights of Assembly, Instruction, and Petition

Article 33. Excessive Bail, Fines, and Punishments Prohibited

Article 34. Martial Law Limited

Article 35. The Judiciary; Tenure of Office, Etc

Article 36. Pensions

Article 36-A. Use of Retirement Funds

Article 37. Separation of Powers

Article 38. Social Virtues Inculcated

Article 39. Changes in Town and City Charters; Referendum Required

PART SECOND --- FORM OF GOVERNMENT

Name of Body Politic – Page 25

Article 1. Name of Body Politic

General Court – Page 26

Article 2. Legislature, How Constituted

Article 3. General Court, When to Meet and Dissolve

Article 4. Power of General Court to Establish Courts

Article 5. Power to Make Laws, Elect Officers, Define Their Powers and Duties, Impose Fines, and Assess Taxes; Prohibited From Authorizing Towns to Aid Certain Corporations

Article 5-A. Continuity of Government in Case of Enemy Attack

Article 5-B. Power to Provide For Tax Valuations Based On Use

Article 6. Valuation and Taxation

Article 6-A. Use of Certain Revenues Restricted to Highways

Article 6-B. Use of Lottery Revenues Restricted to Educational Purposes

Article 7. Members of Legislature not to Take Fees Or Act As Counsel

Article 8. Open Sessions of Legislature

HOUSE OF REPRESENTATIVES – Page 31

Article 9. Representatives Elected Every Second Year; Apportionment of Representatives

Article 9-A. Legislative Adjustments of Census With Reference to Non-Residents

Article 10. Repealed

Article 11. Small Towns, Representation by Districts and Floterial Districts

Article 11-A. Division of Town, Ward, Or Place; Representative Districts

Article 12. Biennial Election of Representatives in November

Article 13. Repealed

Article 14. Representatives, How Elected, Qualifications of

Article 15. Compensation of The Legislature

Article 16. Vacancies in House, How Filled

Article 17. House to Impeach Before The Senate

Article 18. Money Bills to Originate in House

Article 18-A. Budget Bills

Article 19. Adjournment

Article 20. Quorum, What Constitutes

Article 21. Privileges of Members of The Legislature

Article 22. House to Elect Speaker and Officers, Settle Rules of Proceedings, and Punish Misconduct

Article 23. Senate and Executive Have Like Powers; Imprisonment Limited

Article 24. Journals and Laws to be Published; Yeas and Nays, and Protests

SENATE – Page 37

Article 25. Senate; How Constituted

Article 26. Senatorial Districts, How Constituted

Article 26-A. Division of Town, Ward, Or Lace; Senatorial Districts

Article 27. Election of Senators

Article 28. Repealed

Article 29. Qualifications of Senators

Article 30. Inhabitant Defined

Article 31. Inhabitants of Unincorporated Places; Their Rights, Etc

Article 32. Biennial Meetings, How Warned, Governed, and Conducted; Return of Votes, Etc

Article 33. Secretary of State to Count Votes For Senators and Notify Persons Elected

Article 34. Vacancies in Senate, How Filled

8

Article 35. Senate, Judges of Their Own Elections

Article 36. Adjournment

Article 37. Senate to Elect Their Own Officers; Quorum

Article 38. Senate to Try Impeachments; Mode of Proceeding

Article 39. Judgment On Impeachment Limited

Article 40. Chief Justice to Preside On Impeachment of Governor

EXECUTIVE POWER – GOVERNOR – Page 42

Article 41. Governor, Supreme Executive Magistrate

Article 42. Election of Governor, Return of Votes; Electors; If No Choice, Legislature to Elect One of Two Highest Candidates; Qualifications For Governor

Article 43. in Cases of Disagreement, Governor to Adjourn Or Prorogue Legislature; If Causes Exist, May Convene Them Elsewhere

Article 44. Veto to Bills

Article 45. Resolves to be Treated Like Bills

Article 46. Nomination and Appointment of Officers

Article 47. Governor and Council Have Negative On Each Other

Article 48. Repealed

Article 49. President of Senate, Etc. to Act As Governor When Office Vacant; Speaker of House to Act When Office of President of Senate Also Vacant

Article 49-A. Prolonged Failure to Qualify; Vacancy in Office of Governor Due to Physical Or Mental Incapacity, Etc

Article 50. Governor to Prorogue Or Adjourn Legislature, and Call Extra Sessions

Article 51. Powers and Duties of Governor As Commander-in-Chief

Article 52. Pardoning Power

Article 53. Repealed

Article 54. Repealed

Article 55. Repealed

Article 56. Disbursements From Treasury

Article 57. Repealed

Article 58. Compensation of Governor and Council

Article 59. Salaries of Judges

COUNCIL – Page 50

Article 60. Councilors; Mode of Election, Etc

Article 61. Vacancies, How Filled, If No Choice

Article 62. Subsequent Vacancies; Governor to Convene; Duties

Article 63. Impeachment of Councilors

Article 64. Secretary to Record Proceedings of Council

Article 65. Councilor Districts Provided For

Article 66. Elections by Legislature May be Adjourned From Day to Day; Order Thereof

SECRETARY, TREASURER, ETC. – Page 53

Article 67. Election of Secretary and Treasurer

Article 68. State Records, Where Kept; Duty of Secretary

Article 69. Deputy Secretary

Article 70. Secretary to Give Bond

COUNTY TREASURER, ETC. – Page 54

Article 71. County Treasurers, Registers of Probate, County Attorneys, Sheriffs, and Registers of Deeds Elected

Article 72. Counties May be Divided Into Districts For Registering Deeds

JUDICIARY POWER – Page 55

Article 72-A. Supreme and Superior Courts

Article 73. Tenure of Office to be Expressed in Commissions; Judges to Hold Office During Good Behavior, Etc.; Removal

Article 73-A. Supreme Court, Administration

Article 74. Judges to Give Opinions, When

Article 75. Justices of Peace Commissioned For Five Years

Article 76. Divorce and Probate Appeals, Where Tried

Article 77. Jurisdiction of Justices in Civil Causes

Article 78. Judges and Sheriffs, When Disqualified by Age

Article 79. Judges and Justices not to Act As Counsel

Article 80. Jurisdiction and Term of Probate Courts

Article 81. Judges and Registers of Probate not to Act As Counsel

CLERKS OF COURTS – Page 58

Article 82. Clerks of Courts, by Whom Appointed

ENCOURAGEMENT OF LITERATURE, TRADE, ETC. – Page 59

Article 83. Encouragement of Literature, Etc.; Control of Corporations, Monopolies, Etc

OATHS AND SUBSCRIPTIONS EXCLUSION FROM OFFICES, ETC. – Page 61

Article 84. Oath of Civil Officers

Article 85. Before Whom Taken

Article 86. Form of Commissions

Article 87. Form of Writs

Article 88. Form of Indictments, Etc

Article 89. Suicides and Deodands

Article 90. Existing Laws Continued If not Repugnant

Article 91. Habeas Corpus

Article 92. Enacting Style of Statutes

Article 93. Governor and Judges Prohibited From Holding Other Offices

Article 94. Incompatibility of Offices; Only Two Offices of Profit to be Holden At Same Time

Article 95. Incompatibility of Certain Offices

Article 96. Bribery and Corruption Disqualify For Office

Article 97. Repealed

Article 98. Constitution, When to Take Effect

Article 99. Repealed

Article 100. Alternate Methods of Proposing Amendments

Article 101. Enrollment of Constitution

PART FIRST- BILL OF RIGHTS

Article 1. Equality of Men; Origin and Object of Government

All men are born equally free and independent; therefore, all government of right originates from the people, is founded in consent, and instituted for the general good.

Article 2. Natural Rights

All men have certain natural, essential, and inherent rights - among which are, the enjoying and defending life and liberty; acquiring, possessing, and protecting, property; and, in a word, of seeking and obtaining happiness. Equality of rights under the law shall not be denied or abridged by this state on account of race, creed, color, sex or national origin.

Article 2-a. The Bearing of Arms

All persons have the right to keep and bear arms in defense of themselves, their families, their property and the state.

Article 3. Society, its Organization and Purposes

When men enter into a state of society, they surrender up some of their natural rights to that society, in order to ensure the protection of others; and, without such an equivalent, the surrender is void.

Article 4. Rights of Conscience Unalienable

Among the natural rights, some are, in their very nature unalienable, because no equivalent can be given or received for them. of this kind are the Rights of Conscience.

Article 5. Religious Freedom Recognized

Every individual has a natural and unalienable right to worship God according to the dictates of his own conscience, and reason; and no subject shall be hurt, molested, or restrained, in his peers on, liberty, or estate, for worshipping God in the manner and season most agreeable to the dictates of his own conscience; or for his religious profession, sentiments, or persuasion; provided he doth not disturb the public peace or disturb others in their religious worship.

Article 6. Morality and Piety

As morality and piety, rightly grounded on high principles, will give the best and greatest security to government, and will lay, in the hearts of men, the strongest obligations to due subjection; and as the knowledge of these is most likely to be propagated through a society, therefore, the several parishes, bodies, corporate, or religious societies shall at all times have the right of electing their own teachers, and of contracting with them for their support or maintenance, or both. But no person shall ever be compelled to pay towards the support of the schools of any sect or denomination. and every person, denomination or sect shall be equally under the protection of the law; and no subordination of any one sect, denomination or persuasion to another shall ever be established.

Article 7. State Sovereignty

The people of this state have the sole and exclusive right of governing themselves as a free, sovereign, and independent state; and do, and forever hereafter shall, exercise and enjoy every power, jurisdiction, and right, pertaining thereto, which is not, or may not hereafter be, by them expressly delegated to the United States of America in congress assembled.

Article 8. Accountability of Magistrates and Officers; Public's Right to Know

All power residing originally in, and being derived from, the people, all the magistrates and officers of government are their substitutes and agents, and at all times accountable to them. Government, therefore, should be open, accessible, accountable and responsive. to that end, the public's right of access to governmental proceedings and records shall not be unreasonably restricted.

Article 9. No Hereditary Office or Place

No office or place, whatsoever, in government, shall be hereditary - the abilities and integrity requisite in all, not being transmissible to posterity or relations.

Article 10. Right of Revolution

Government being instituted for the common benefit, protection, and security, of the whole community, and not for the private interest or emolument of any one man, family, or class of men; therefore, whenever the ends of government are perverted, and public liberty manifestly endangered, and all other means of redress are ineffectual, the people may, and of right ought to reform the old, or establish a new government. The doctrine of nonresistance against arbitrary power, and oppression, is absurd, slavish, and destructive of the good and happiness of mankind.

Article 11. Elections and Elective Franchises

All elections are to be free, and every inhabitant of the state of 18 years of age and upwards shall have an equal right to vote in any election. Every person shall be considered an inhabitant for the purposes of voting in the town, ward, or unincorporated place where he has his domicile. No person shall have the right to vote under the constitution of this state who has been convicted of treason, bribery or any willful violation of the election laws of this state or of the United States; but the supreme court may, on notice to the attorney general, restore the privilege to vote to any person who may have forfeited it by conviction of such offenses. The general court shall provide by law for voting by qualified voters who at the time of the biennial or state elections, or of the primary elections therefor, or of city elections, or of town elections by official ballot, are absent from the city or town of which they are inhabitants, or who by reason of physical disability are unable to vote in person, in the choice of any officer or officers to be elected or upon any question submitted at such election. Voting registration and polling places shall be easily accessible to all persons including disabled and elderly persons who are otherwise qualified to vote in the choice of any officer or officers to be elected or upon any question submitted at such election. The right to vote shall not be denied to any person because of the non-payment of any tax. Every inhabitant of the state, having the proper qualifications, has equal right to be elected into office.

Article 12. Protection and Taxation Reciprocal

Every member of the community has a right to be protected by it, in the enjoyment of his life, liberty, and property; he is therefore bound to contribute his share in the expense of such protection, and to yield his personal service when necessary. But no part of a man's property shall be taken from him, or applied to public uses, without his own consent, or that of the representative body of the people. Nor are the inhabitants of this state controllable by any other laws than those to which they, or their representative body, have given their consent.

Article 12-a. Power to Take Property Limited

No part of a person's property shall be taken by eminent domain and transferred, directly or indirectly, to another person if the taking is for the purpose of private development or other private use of the property.

Article 13. Conscientious Objectors not Compelled to Bear Arms

No person, who is conscientiously scrupulous about the lawfulness of bearing arms, shall be compelled thereto.

Article 14. Legal Remedies to be Free, Complete, and Prompt

Every subject of this state is entitled to a certain remedy, by having recourse to the laws, for all injuries he may receive in his person, property, or character; to obtain right and justice freely, without being obliged to purchase it; completely, and without any denial; promptly, and without delay; conformably to the laws.

Article 15. Right of Accused

No subject shall be held to answer for any crime, or offense, until the same is fully and plainly, substantially and formally, described to him; or be compelled to accuse or furnish evidence against himself. Every subject shall have a right to produce all proofs that may be favorable to himself; to meet the witnesses against him face to face, and to be fully heard in his defense, by himself, and counsel. No subject shall be arrested, imprisoned, despoiled, or deprived of his property, immunities, or privileges, put out of the protection of the law, exiled or deprived of his life, liberty, or estate, but by the judgment of his peers, or the law of the land; provided that, in any proceeding to commit a person acquitted of a criminal charge by reason of insanity, due process shall require that clear and convincing evidence that the person is potentially dangerous to himself or to others and that the person suffers from a mental disorder must be established. Every person held to answer in any crime or offense punishable by deprivation of liberty shall have the right to counsel at the expense of the state if need is shown; this right he is at liberty to waive, but only after the matter has been thoroughly explained by the court.

Article 16. Former Jeopardy; Jury Trial in Capital Cases

No subject shall be liable to be tried, after an acquittal, for the same crime or offense. Nor shall the legislature make any law that shall subject any person to a capital punishment, (excepting for the government of the army and navy, and the militia in actual service) without trial by jury.

Article 17. Venue of Criminal Prosecutions

in criminal prosecutions, the trial of facts, in the vicinity where they happened, is so essential to the security of the life, liberty and estate of the citizen, that no crime or offense ought to be tried in any other county or judicial district than that in which it is committed; except in any case in any particular county or judicial district, upon motion by the defendant, and after a finding by the court that a fair and impartial trial cannot be had where the offense may be committed, the court shall direct the trial to a county or judicial district in which a fair and impartial trial can be obtained.

Article 18. Penalties to be Proportioned to Offenses; True Design of Punishment

All penalties ought to be proportioned to the nature of the offense. No wise legislature will affix the same punishment to the crimes of theft, forgery , and the like, which they do to those of murder and treason. Where the same undistinguishing severity is exerted against all offenses, the people are led to forget the real distinction in the crimes themselves, and to commit the most flagrant with as little compunction as they do the lightest offenses. For the same reason a multitude of sanguinary laws is both impolitic and unjust. The true design of all punishments being to reform, not to exterminate mankind.

Article 19. Searches and Seizures Regulated

Every subject hath a right to be secure from all unreasonable searches and seizures of his person, his houses, his papers, and all his possessions. Therefore, all warrants to search suspected places, or arrest a person for examination or trial in prosecutions for criminal matters, are contrary to this right, if the cause or foundation of them be not previously supported by oath or affirmation; and if the order, in a warrant to a civil officer, to make search in suspected places, or to arrest one or more suspected persons or to seize their property, be not accompanied with a special designation of the persons or objects of search, arrest, or seizure; and no warrant ought to be issued; but in cases and with the formalities, prescribed by law.

Article 20. Jury Trial in Civil Causes

in all controversies concerning property, and in all suits between two or more persons except those in which another practice is and has been customary and except those in which the value in controversy does not exceed $1,500 and no title to real estate is involved, the parties have a right to a trial by jury. This method of procedure shall be held sacred, unless, in cases* arising on the high seas and in cases relating to mariners' wages, the legislature shall think it necessary hereafter to alter it.

Article 21. Jurors; Compensation

in order to reap the fullest advantage of the inestimable privilege of the trial by jury, great care ought to be taken, that none but qualified persons should be appointed to serve; and such ought to be fully compensated for their travel, time and attendance.

Article 22. Free Speech; Liberty of the Press

Free speech and liberty of the press are essential to the security of freedom in a state: They ought, therefore, to be inviolably preserved.

Article 23. Retrospective Laws Prohibited

Retrospective laws are highly injurious, oppressive, and unjust. No such laws, therefore, should be made, either for the decision of civil causes, or the punishment of offenses.

Article 24. Militia

A well regulated militia is the proper, natural, and sure defense, of a state.

Article 25. Standing Armies

Standing armies are dangerous to liberty, and ought not to be raised, or kept up, without the consent of the legislature.

Article 26. Military Subject to Civil Power

in all cases, and at all times, the military ought to be under strict subordination to, and governed by, the civil power.

Article 27. Quartering of Soldiers

No soldier in time of peace, shall be quartered in any house, without the consent of the owner; and in time of war, such quarters ought not to be made but by the civil authorities in a manner ordained by the legislature.

Article 28. Taxes, by Whom Levied

No subsidy, charge, tax, impost, or duty, shall be established, fixed, laid, or levied, under any pretext whatsoever, without the consent of the people, or their representatives in the legislature, or authority derived from that body.

Article 28-a. Mandated Programs

The state shall not mandate or assign any new, expanded or modified programs or responsibilities to any political subdivision in such a way as to necessitate additional local expenditures by the political subdivision unless such programs or responsibilities are fully funded by the state or unless such programs or responsibilities are approved for funding by a vote of the local legislative body of the political subdivision.

Article 29. Suspension of Laws by Legislature Only

The power of suspending the laws, or the execution of them, ought never to be exercised but by the legislature, or by authority derived therefrom, to be exercised in such particular cases only as the legislature shall expressly provide for.

Article 30. Freedom of Speech

The freedom of deliberation, speech, and debate, in either house of the legislature, is so essential to the rights of the people, that it cannot be the foundation of any action, complaint, or prosecution, in any other court or place whatsoever.

Article 31. Meetings of Legislature, for What Purposes

The legislature shall assemble for the redress of public grievances and for making such laws as the public good may require.

Article 32. Rights of Assembly, Instruction, and Petition

The people have a right, in an orderly and peaceable manner, to assemble and consult upon the common good, give instructions to their representatives, and to request of the legislative body, by way of petition or remonstrance, redress of the wrongs done them, and of the grievances they suffer.

Article 33. Excessive Bail, Fines, and Punishments Prohibited

No magistrate, or court of law, shall demand excessive bail or sureties, impose excessive fines, or inflict cruel or unusual punishments.

Article 34. Martial Law Limited

No person can, in any case, be subjected to law martial, or to any pains or penalties by virtue of that law, except those employed in the army or navy, and except the militia in actual service, but by authority of the legislature.

Article 35. The Judiciary; Tenure of Office, etc

It is essential to the preservation of the rights of every individual, his life, liberty, property, and character, that there be an impartial interpretation of the laws, and administration of justice. It is the right of every citizen to be tried by judges as impartial as the lot of humanity will admit. It is therefore not only the best policy, but for the security of the rights of the people, that the judges of the supreme judicial court should hold their offices so long as they behave well; subject, however, to such limitations, on account of age, as may be provided by the constitution of the state; and that they should have honorable salaries, ascertained and established by standing laws.

Article 36. Pensions

Economy being a most essential virtue in all states, especially in a young one, no pension shall be granted, but in consideration of actual services; and such pensions ought to be granted with great caution, by the legislature, and never for more than one year at a time.

Article 36-a Use of Retirement Funds

The employer contributions certified as payable to the New Hampshire retirement system or any successor system to fund the system's liabilities, as shall be determined by sound actuarial valuation and practice, independent of the executive office, shall be appropriated each fiscal year to the same extent as is certified. All of the assets and proceeds, and income there from, of the New Hampshire retirement system and of any and all other retirement systems for public officers and employees operated by the state or by any of its political subdivisions, and of any successor system, and all contributions and payments made to any such system to provide for retirement and related benefits shall be held, invested or disbursed as in trust for the exclusive purpose of providing for such benefits and shall not be encumbered for, or diverted to, any other purposes.

Article 37. Separation of Powers

in the government of this state, the three essential powers thereof, to wit, the legislative, executive, and judicial, ought to be kept as separate from, and independent of, each other, as the nature of a free government will admit, or as is consistent with that chain of connection that binds the whole fabric of the constitution in one indissoluble bond of union and amity.

Article 38. Social Virtues Inculcated

A frequent recurrence to the fundamental principles of the constitution, and a constant adherence to justice, moderation, temperance, industry, frugality, and all the social virtues, are indispensably necessary to preserve the blessings of liberty and good government; the people ought, therefore, to have a particular regard to all those principles in the choice of their officers and representatives, and they have a right to require of their lawgivers and magistrates, an exact and constant observance of them, in the formation and execution of the laws necessary for the good administration of government.

Article 39. Changes in Town and City Charters, Referendum Required

No law changing the charter or form of government of a particular city or town shall be enacted by the legislature except to become effective upon the approval of the voters of such city or town upon a referendum to be provided for in said law. The legislature may by general law authorize cities and towns to adopt or amend their charters or forms of government in any way which is not in conflict with general law, provided that such charters or amendments shall become effective only upon the approval of the voters of each such city or town on a referendum.

PART SECOND --- FORM OF GOVERNMENT

Name of Body Politic

Article 1. Name of Body Politic

The people inhabiting the territory formerly called the province of New Hampshire, do hereby solemnly and mutually agree with each other, to form themselves into a free, sovereign and independent body-politic, or state, by the name of the State of New Hampshire.

GENERAL COURT

Article 2. Legislature, How Constituted

The supreme legislative power, within this state, shall be vested in the senate and house of representatives, each of which shall have a negative on the other.

Article 3. General Court, When to Meet and Dissolve

The senate and house shall assemble biennially on the first Wednesday of December for organizational purposes in even numbered years, and shall assemble annually on the first Wednesday following the first Tuesday in January, and at such other times as they may judge necessary; and shall dissolve and be dissolved at 12:01 A.M. on the first Wednesday of December in even numbered years and shall be styled The General Court of New Hampshire.

Article 4. Power of General Court to Establish Courts

The general court (except as otherwise provided by Article 72-a of Part 2) shall forever have full power and authority to erect and constitute judicatories and courts of record, or other courts, to beholden, in the name of the state, for the hearing, trying, and determining, all manner of crimes, offenses, pleas, processes, plaints, action, causes, matters and things whatsoever arising or happening within this state, or between or concerning persons inhabiting or residing, or brought, within the same, whether the same be criminal or civil, or whether the crimes be capital, or not capital, and whether the said pleas be real, personal or mixed, and for the awarding and issuing execution thereon. to which courts and judicatories, are hereby given and granted, full power and authority, from time to time, to administer oaths or affirmations, for the better discovery of truth in any matter in controversy, or depending before them.

Article 5. Power to Make Laws, Elect Officers, Define Their Powers and Duties, Impose Fines and Assess Taxes; Prohibited from Authorizing Towns to Aid Certain Corporations

and farther, full power and authority are hereby given and granted to the said general court, from time to time, to make, ordain, and establish, all manner of wholesome and reasonable orders, laws, statutes, ordinances, directions, and instructions, either with penalties, or without, so as the same be not repugnant or contrary to this constitution, as they may judge for the benefit and welfare of this state, and for the governing and ordering thereof, and of the subjects of the same, for the necessary support and defense of the government thereof, and to name and settle biennially, or provide by fixed laws for the naming and settling, all civil officers within this state, such officers excepted, the election and appointment of whom are hereafter in this form of government otherwise provided for; and to set forth the several duties, powers, and limits, of the several civil and military officers of this state, and the forms of such oaths or affirmations as shall be respectively administered unto them, for the execution of their several offices and places, so as the same be not repugnant or contrary to this constitution; and also to impose fines, mulcts, imprisonments, and other punishments, and to impose and levy proportional and reasonable assessments, rates, and taxes, upon all the inhabitants of, and residents within, the said state; and upon all estates within the same; to be issued and disposed of by warrant, under the hand of the governor of this state for the time being, with the advice and consent of the council, for the public service, in the necessary defense and support of the government of this state, and the protection and preservation of the subjects thereof, according to such acts as are, or shall be, in force within the same; provided that the general court shall not authorize any town to loan or give its money or credit directly or indirectly for the benefit of any corporation having for its object a dividend of profits or in any way aid the same by taking its stocks or bonds. For the purpose of encouraging conservation of the forest resources of the state, the general court may provide for special assessments, rates and taxes on growing wood and timber.

Article 5-a. Continuity of Government in Case of Enemy Attack

Notwithstanding any general or special provision of this constitution, the general court, in order to insure continuity of state and local government operations in periods of emergency resulting from disasters caused by enemy attack, shall have the power and the immediate duty to provide for prompt and temporary succession to the powers and duties of public offices, of whatever nature and whether filled by election or appointment, the incumbents of which may become unavailable for carrying on the powers and duties of such offices, and to adopt such other measures as may be necessary and proper for insuring the continuity of governmental operations including but not limited to the financing thereof. in the exercise of the powers hereby conferred the general court shall in all respects conform to the requirements of this constitution except to the extent that in the judgment of the general court so to do would be impracticable or would admit of undue delay.

Article 5-b. Power to Provide for Tax Valuations Based on Use

 The general court may provide for the assessment of any class of real estate at valuations based upon the current use thereof.

Article 6. Valuation and Taxation

The public charges of government, or any part thereof, may be raised by taxation upon polls, estates, and other classes of property, including franchises and property when passing by will or inheritance; and there shall be a valuation of the estates within the state taken anew once in every five years, at least, and as much oftener as the general court shall order.

June 2, 1784 Amended 1903 to permit taxes on other classes of property including franchises and property passing by inheritances.

Article 6-a. Use of Certain Revenues Restricted to Highways

All revenue in excess of the necessary cost of collection and administration accruing to the state from registration fees, operators' licenses, gasoline road tolls or any other special charges or taxes with respect to the operation of motor vehicles or the sale or consumption of motor vehicle fuels shall be appropriated and used exclusively for the construction, reconstruction and maintenance of public highways within this state, including the supervision of traffic thereon and payment of the interest and principal of obligations incurred for said purposes; and no part of such revenues shall, by transfer of funds or otherwise, be diverted to any other purpose whatsoever.

Article 6-b. Use of Lottery Revenues Restricted to Educational Purposes

All moneys received from a state-run lottery and all the interest received on such moneys shall, after deducting the necessary costs of administration, be appropriated and used exclusively for the school districts of the state. Such moneys shall be used exclusively for the purpose of state aid to education and shall not be transferred or diverted to any other purpose.

Article 7. Members of Legislature not to Take Fees or Act as Counsel

No member of the general court shall take fees, be of counsel, or act as advocate, in any cause before either branch of the legislature; and upon due proof thereof, such member shall forfeit his seat in the legislature.

Article 8. Open Sessions of Legislature

The doors of the galleries, of each house of the legislature, shall be kept open to all persons who behave decently, except when the welfare of the state, in the opinion of either branch, shall require secrecy.

House of Representatives

Article 9. Representatives Elected Every Second Year; Apportionment of Representatives

There shall be in the legislature of this state a house of representatives, biennially elected and founded on principles of equality, and representation therein shall be as equal as circumstances will admit. The whole number of representatives to be chosen from the towns, wards, places, and representative districts thereof established hereunder, shall be not less than three hundred seventy-five or more than four hundred. As soon as possible after the convening of the next regular session of the legislature, and at the session in 1971, and every ten years thereafter, the legislature shall make an apportionment of representatives according to the last general census of the inhabitants of the state taken by authority of the United States or of this state. in making such apportionment, no town, ward or place shall be divided nor the boundaries thereof altered.

Article 9-a. Legislative Adjustments of Census with Reference to Non-Residents

The general court shall have the power to provide by statute for making suitable adjustments to the general census of the inhabitants of the state taken by the authority of the United States or of this state on account of non-residents temporarily residing in this state.

Article 10. Representation of Small Towns

Repealed.

Article 11. Small Towns; Representation by Districts

When the population of any town or ward, according to the last federal census, is within a reasonable deviation from the ideal population for one or more representative seats, the town or ward shall have its own district of one or more representative seats. The apportionment shall not deny any other town or ward membership in one non-floterial representative district. When any town, ward, or unincorporated place has fewer than the number of inhabitants necessary to entitle it to one representative, the legislature shall form those towns, wards, or unincorporated places into representative districts which contain a sufficient number of inhabitants to entitle each district so formed to one or more representatives for the entire district. in forming the districts, the boundaries of towns, wards, and unincorporated places shall be preserved and contiguous. The excess number of inhabitants of district may be added to the excess number of inhabitants of other districts to form at-large or floterial districts conforming to acceptable deviations. The legislature shall form the representative districts at the regular session following every decennial federal census.

Article 11-a. Division of Town, Ward or Place; Representative Districts

Notwithstanding Articles 9 and 11, a law providing for an apportionment to form representative districts under Articles 9 and 11 of Part Second may divide a town, ward or unincorporated place into two or more representative districts if such town, ward or place, by referendum requests such division.

Article 12. Biennial Election of Representatives in November

The members of the house of representatives shall be chosen biennially, in the month of November, and shall be the second branch of the legislature.

Article 13. Qualifications of Electors

Repealed.

Article 14. Representatives, How Elected, Qualifications of

Every member of the house of representatives shall be chosen by ballot; and, for two years, at least, next preceding his election shall have been an inhabitant of this state; shall be, at the time of his election, an inhabitant of the town, ward, place, or district he may be chosen to represent and shall cease to represent such town, ward, place, or district immediately on his ceasing to be qualified as aforesaid.

Article 15. Compensation of the Legislature

The presiding officers of both houses of the legislature, shall severally receive out of the state treasury as compensation in full for their services for the term elected the sum of $250, and all other members thereof, seasonably attending and not departing without license, the sum of $200 and each member shall receive mileage for actual daily attendance on legislative days, but not after the legislature shall have been in session for 45 legislative days or after the first day of July following the annual assembly of the legislature, whichever occurs first; provided, however, that, when a special session shall be called by the governor or by a 2/3 vote of the then qualified members of each branch of the general court, such officers and members shall receive for attendance an additional compensation of $3 per day for a period not exceeding 15 days and the usual mileage. Nothing herein shall prevent the payment of additional mileage to members attending committee meetings or on other legislative business on nonlegislative days.

Article 16. Vacancies in House, How Filled

All intermediate vacancies, in the house of representatives may be filled up, from time to time, in the same manner as biennial elections are made.

Article 17. House to Impeach Before the Senate

The house of representatives shall be the grand inquest of the state; and all impeachments made by them, shall be heard and tried by the senate.

Article 18. Money Bills to Originate in House

All money bills shall originate in the house of representatives; but the senate may propose, or concur with amendments, as on other bills.

Article 18-a Budget Bills

All sections of all budget bills before the general court shall contain only the operating and capital expenses for the executive, legislative and judicial branches of government. No section or footnote of any such budget bill shall contain any provision which establishes, amends or repeals statutory law, other than provisions establishing, amending or repealing operating and capital expenses for the executive, legislative and judicial branches of government.

Article 19. Adjournment

The house of representatives shall have the power to adjourn themselves.

Article 20. Quorum, What Constitutes

A majority of the members of the house of representatives shall be a quorum for doing business: But when less than two-thirds of the representatives elected shall be present, the assent of two-thirds of those members shall be necessary to render their acts and proceedings valid.

Article 21. Privileges of Members of Legislature

No member of the house of representatives, or senate shall be arrested, or held to bail, on mesne process, during his going to, returning from, or attendance upon, the court.

Article 22. House to Elect Speaker and Officers, Settle Rules of Proceedings, and Punish Misconduct

The house of representatives shall choose their own speaker, appoint their own officers, and settle the rules of proceedings in their own house; and shall be judge of the returns, elections, and qualifications, of its members, as pointed out in this constitution. They shall have authority to punish, by imprisonment, every person who shall be guilty of disrespect to the house, in its presence, by any disorderly and contemptuous behavior, or by threatening, or ill treating, any of its members; or by obstructing its deliberations; every person guilty of a breach of its privileges, in making arrests for debt, or by assaulting any member during his attendance at any session; in assaulting or disturbing any one of its officers in the execution of any order or procedure of the house; in assaulting any witness, or other person, ordered to attend, by and during his attendance of the house; or in rescuing any person arrested by order of the house, knowing them to be such.

Article 23. Senate and Executive Have Like Powers; Imprisonment Limited

The senate, governor and council, shall have the same powers in like cases; provided, that no imprisonment by either, for any offense, exceeds ten days.

Article 24 Journals and Laws to be Published; Yeas and Nayes; and Protests

The journals of the proceedings, and all public acts of both houses, of the legislature, shall be printed and published immediately after every adjournment or prorogation; and upon motion made by any one member, duly seconded, the yeas and nays, upon any question, shall be entered, on the journal. and any member of the senate, or house of representatives, shall have a right, on motion made at the time for t hat purpose to have his protest, or dissent, with the reasons, against any vote, resolve, or bill passed, entered on the journal.

Senate

Article 25. Senate, How Constituted

The senate shall consist of twenty-four members.

Article 26. Senatorial Districts, How Constituted

and that the state may be equally represented in the senate, the legislature shall divide the state into single-member districts, as nearly equal as may be in population, each consisting of contiguous towns, city wards and unincorporated places, without dividing any town, city ward or unincorporated place. The legislature shall form the single-member districts at its next session after approval of this article by the voters of the state and thereafter at the regular session following each decennial federal census.

Article 26-a. Division of Town, Ward or Place; Senatorial Districts

Notwithstanding Article 26 or any other article, a law providing for an apportionment to form senatorial districts under Article 26 of Part Second may divide a town, ward or unincorporated place into two or more senatorial districts if such town, ward or place by referendum requests such division.

Article 27. Election of Senators

The freeholders and other inhabitants of each district, qualified as in this constitution is provided shall biennially give in their votes for a senator, at some meeting holden in the month of November.

Article 28. Senators, How and by Whom Chosen; Right of Suffrage

Repealed.

Article 29. Qualifications of Senators

Provided nevertheless, that no person shall be capable of being elected a senator, who is not of the age of thirty years, and who shall not have been an inhabitant of this state for seven years immediately preceding his election, and at the time thereof he shall be an inhabitant of the district for which he shall be chosen. Should such person, after election, cease to be an inhabitant of the district for which he was chosen, he shall be disqualified to hold said position and a vacancy shall be declared therein.

Article 30. Inhabitant Defined

and every person, qualified as the constitution provides, shall be considered an inhabitant for the purpose of being elected into any office or place within this state, in the town, or ward, where he is domiciled.

Article 31. Inhabitants of Unincorporated Places; Their Rights, etc

Repealed.

Article 32. Biennial Meetings, How Warned, Governed, and Conducted; Return of Votes, etc

The meetings for the choice of governor, council and senators, shall be warned by warrant from the selectmen, and governed by a moderator, who shall, in the presence of the selectmen (whose duty it shall be to attend) in open meeting, receive the votes of all the inhabitants of such towns and wards present, and qualified to vote for senators; and shall, in said meetings, in presence of the said selectmen, and of the town or city clerk, in said meetings, sort and count the said votes, and make a public declaration thereof, with the name of every person voted for, and the number of votes for each person; and the town or city clerk shall make a fair record of the same at large, in the town book, and shall make out a fair attested copy thereof, to be by him sealed up and directed to the secretary of state, within five days following the election, with a superscription expressing the purport there of.

Article 33. Secretary of State to Count Votes for Senators and Notify Persons Elected

and that there may be a due meeting of senators and representatives on the first Wednesday of December, biennially, the secretary of state shall, as soon as may be, examine the returned copy of such records; and fourteen days before the first Wednesday of December, he shall issue his summons to such persons as appear to be chosen senators and representatives, by a plurality of votes, to attend and take their seats on that day.

Article 34. Vacancies in Senate, How Filled

and in case there shall not appear to be a senator elected, by a plurality of votes, for any district, the deficiency shall be supplied in the following manner, viz. The members of the house of representatives, and such senators as shall be declared elected, shall take the names of the two persons having the highest number of votes in the district, and out of them shall elect, by joint ballot, the senator wanted for such district; and in this manner all such vacancies shall be filled up, in every district of the state and in case the person receiving a plurality of votes in any district is found by the Senate not to be qualified to be seated, a new election shall be held forthwith in said district. All vacancies in the senate arising by death, removal out of the state, or otherwise, except from failure to elect, shall be filled by a new election by the people of the district upon the requisition of the governor and council, as soon as may be after such vacancies shall happen.

Article 35. Senate, Judges of Their Own Elections

The senate shall be final judges of the elections, returns, and qualifications, of their own members, as pointed out in this constitution.

Article 36. Adjournment

The senate shall have power to adjourn themselves, and whenever they shall sit on the trial of any impeachment, they may adjourn to such time and place as they may think proper although the legislature be not assembled on such day, or at such place.

Article 37. Senate to Elect Their Own Officers; Quorum

The senate shall appoint their president and other officers, and determine their own rules of proceedings: and not less than thirteen members of the senate shall make a quorum for doing business; and when less than sixteen senators shall be present, the assent of ten, at least, shall be necessary to render their acts and proceedings valid.

Article 38. Senate to Try Impeachments; Mode of Proceeding

The senate shall be a court, with full power and authority to hear, try, and determine, all impeachments made by the house of representatives against any officer or officers of the state, for bribery, corruption, malpractice or maladministration, in office; with full power to issue summons, or compulsory process, for convening witnesses before them: But previous to the trial of any such impeachment, the members of the senate shall respectively be sworn truly and impartially to try and determine the charge in question, according to evidence. and every officer, impeached for bribery, corruption, malpractice or maladministration in office, shall be served with an attested copy of the impeachment, and order of the senate thereon with such citation as the senate may direct, setting forth the time and place of their sitting to try the impeachment; which service shall be made by the sheriff, or such other sworn officer as the senate may appoint, at least fourteen days previous to the time of trial; and such citation being duly served and returned, the senate may proceed in the hearing of the impeachment, giving the person impeached, if he shall appear, full liberty of producing witnesses and proofs, and of making his defense, by himself and counsel, and may also, upon his refusing or neglecting to appear hear the proofs in support of the impeachment, and render judgment thereon, his nonappearance notwithstanding; and such judgment shall have the same force and effect as if the person impeached had appeared and pleaded in the trial.

Article 39. Judgment on Impeachment Limited

Their judgment, however, shall not extend further than removal from office, disqualification to hold or enjoy any place of honor, trust, or profit, under this state, but the party so convicted, shall nevertheless be liable to indictment, trial, judgment, and punishment, according to the laws of the land.

Article 40. Chief Justice to Preside on Impeachment of Governor

Whenever the governor shall be impeached, the chief justice of the supreme judicial court, shall, during the trial, preside in the senate, but have no vote therein.

Executive Power

Article 41. Governor, Supreme Executive Magistrate

There shall be a supreme executive magistrate, who shall be styled the Governor of the State of New Hampshire, and whose title shall be His Excellency. The executive power of the state is vested in the governor. The governor shall be responsible for the faithful execution of the laws. He may, by appropriate court action or proceeding brought in the name of the state, enforce compliance with any constitutional or legislative mandate, or restrain violation of any constitutional or legislative power, duty, or right, by any officer, department or agency of the state. This authority shall not be construed to authorize any action or proceedings against the legislative or judicial branches.

Article 42. Election of Governor, Return of Votes; Electors; If No Choice, Legislature to Elect One of Two Highest Candidates; Qualifications for Governor

The governor shall be chosen biennially in the month of November; and the votes for governor shall be received, sorted, counted, certified and returned, in the same manner as the votes for senators; and the secretary shall lay the same before the senate and house of representatives, on the first Wednesday following the first Tuesday of January to be by them examined, and in case of an election by a plurality of votes through the state, the choice shall be by them declared and published. and the qualifications of electors of the governor shall be the same as those for senators; and if no person shall have a plurality of votes, the senate and house of representatives shall, by joint ballot elect one of the two persons, having the highest number of votes, who shall be declared governor. and no person shall be eligible to this office, unless at the time of his election, he shall have been an inhabitant of this state for 7 years next preceding, and unless he shall be of the age of 30 years.

Article 43. in Cases of Disagreement Governor to Adjourn or Prorogue Legislature; If Causes Exist, May Convene Them Elsewhere

in cases of disagreement between the two houses, with regard to the time or place of adjournment or prorogation, the governor, with advice of council, shall have a right to adjourn or prorogue the general court, not exceeding ninety days at any one time, as he may determine the public good may require, and he shall dissolve the same on the first Wednesday of December biennially. and, in cases whereby dangers may arise to the health or lives of the members from their attendance at the general court at any place, the governor may direct the session to be holden at some other the most convenient place within the state.

Article 44. Veto to Bills

Every bill which shall have passed both houses of the general court, shall, before it becomes a law, be presented to the governor, if he approves, he shall sign it, but if not, he shall return it, with his objections, to that house in which it shall have originated, who shall enter the objections at large on their journal, and proceed to reconsider it; if after such reconsideration, two-thirds of that house shall agree to pass the bill, it shall be sent, together with such objections, to the other house, by which it shall likewise be reconsidered, and, if approved by two-thirds of that house, it shall become a law. But in all such cases the votes of both houses shall be determined by yeas and nays, and the names of persons, voting for or against the bill, shall be entered on the journal of each house respectively. If any bill shall not be returned by the governor within five days (Sundays excepted) after it shall have been presented to him, the same shall be a law in like manner as if he had signed it unless the legislature, by their adjournment, prevent its return, in which case it shall not be a law.

Article 45. Resolves to be Treated Like Bills

Every resolve shall be presented to the governor, and before the same shall take effect, shall be approved by him, or being disapproved by him, shall be repassed by the senate and house of representatives, according to the rules and limitations prescribed in the case of a bill.

Article 46. Nomination and Appointment of Officers

All judicial officers, the attorney general, and all officers of the navy, and general and field officers of the militia, shall be nominated and appointed by the governor and council; and every such nomination shall be made at least three days prior to such appointment; and no appointment shall take place, unless a majority of the council agree thereto.

Article 47. Governor and Council Have Negative on Each Other

The governor and council shall have a negative on each other, both in the nominations and appointments. Every nomination and appointment shall be signed by the governor and council, and every negative shall be also signed by the governor or council who made the same.

Article 48. Field Officers to Recommend, and Governor to Appoint, Company Officers

Repealed.

Article 49. President of Senate, etc., to Act as Governor When Office Vacant; Speaker of House to Act When Office of President of Senate Is also Vacant

in the event of the death, resignation, removal from office, failure to qualify, physical or mental incapacity, absence from the state, or other incapacity of the governor, the president of the senate, for the time being, shall act as governor until the vacancy is filled or the incapacity is removed; and if the president of the senate, for any of the above-named causes, shall become incapable of performing the duties of governor, the same shall devolve upon the speaker of the house of representatives, for the time being, or in the case of the like incapacity of the speaker, upon the secretary of state, or in case of his like incapacity, upon the state treasurer, each of whom, in that order, shall act as governor, as herein above provided, until the vacancy is filled or the incapacity removed. Whenever a vacancy for the duration or remainder of the governor´s term of office occurs before the commencement of the last year of such term, a special election for governor shall take place to fill the vacancy, as provided by law. Whenever the speaker of the house acts as governor, he shall act as such only until such time as the vacancy is filled or the incapacity removed in either the office of governor or of president of the senate, whichever occurs first. Whenever either the secretary of state or the treasurer acts as governor, he shall act as such only until such time as the vacancy is filled or the incapacity removed in the offices of governor, of president of the senate or of speaker of the house, whichever occurs first. While acting as governor under this article, the president of the senate, speaker of the house, secretary of state or state treasurer, as the case may be, shall be styled Acting Governor, shall not be required to take an additional oath of office, shall have and exercise all the powers, duties and authorities of, and receive compensation equal to that of the office of governor; and the capacity of each such officer to serve as president of the senate as well as senator, speaker of the house of representatives as well as representative, secretary of state, or state treasurer, as the case may be, or to receive the compensation of such office, shall be suspended only. While the governor or an acting governor is absent from the state on official business, he shall have the power and authority to transact such business.

Article 49-a Prolonged Failure to Qualify; Vacancy in Office of Governor Due to Physical or Mental Incapacity, etc

Whenever the governor transmits to the secretary of state and president of the senate his written declaration that he is unable to discharge the powers and duties of his office by reason of physical or mental incapacity and until he transmits to them a written declaration to the contrary, the president of the senate, for the time being, shall act as governor as provided in article 49, subject to the succession provisions therein set forth. Whenever it reasonably appears to the attorney general and a majority of the council that the governor is unable to discharge the powers and duties of his office by reason of physical or mental incapacity, but the governor is unwilling or unable to transmit his written declaration to such effect as above provided, the attorney general shall file a petition for declaratory judgment in the supreme court requesting a judicial determination of the ability of the governor to discharge the powers and duties of his office. After notice and hearing, the justices of the supreme court shall render such judgment as they find warranted by a preponderance of the evidence; and, if the court holds that the governor is unable to discharge the powers and duties of his office, the president of the senate, for the time being, shall act as governor as provided in article 49, subject to the succession provisions therein set forth, until such time as the disability of the governor is removed or a newly elected governor is inaugurated. Such disability, once determined by the supreme court, may be removed upon petition for declaratory judgment to the supreme court by the governor if the court finds, after notice and hearing, by a preponderance of the evidence that the governor is able to discharge the powers and duties of his office. Whenever such disability of the governor, as determined by his written declaration or by judgment of the supreme court, has continued for a period of 6 months, the general court may, by concurrent resolution adopted by both houses, declare the office of governor vacant. Whenever the governor-elect fails to qualify by reason of physical or mental incapacity or any cause other than death or resignation, for a period of 6 months following the inauguration date established by this constitution, the general court may, by concurrent resolution adopted by both houses, declare the office of governor vacant. The provisions of article 49 shall govern the filling of such vacancy, either by special election or continued service of an acting governor. If the general court is not in session when any such 6-month period expires, the acting governor, upon written request of at least 1/4 of the members of each house, shall convene the general court in special session for the sole purpose of considering and acting on the question whether to declare a vacancy in the office of governor under this article.

Article 50. Governor to Prorogue or Adjourn Legislature, and Call Extra Sessions

The governor, with advice of council, shall have full power and authority, in the recess of the general court, to prorogue the same from time to time, not exceeding ninety days, in any one recess of said court; and during the sessions of said court, to adjourn or prorogue it to any time the two houses may desire, and to call it together sooner than the time to which it may be adjourned, or prorogued, if the welfare of the state should require the same.

Article 51. Powers and Duties of Governor as Commander-in-Chief

The governor of this state for the time being, shall be commander-in-chief of all the military forces of the state; and shall have full power, by himself or by any chief commander, or other officer or officers, from time to time, to train, instruct, exercise and govern the militia; to call forth the militia and to put in warlike posture the inhabitants of the state; to execute the laws of the state and of the United States; to suppress insurrection and to repel invasion; and, in fine, the governor is hereby entrusted with all other powers incident to the office of commander-in-chief to be exercised agreeably to the rules and regulations of the constitution and the laws of the land.

Article 52. Pardoning Power

The power of pardoning offenses, except such as persons may be convicted of before the senate, by impeachment of the house, shall be in the governor, by and with the advice of council: But no charter of pardon, granted by the governor, with advice of the council, before conviction, shall avail the party pleading the same, notwithstanding any general or particular expressions contained therein, descriptive of the offense or offenses intended to be pardoned.

Article 53. Militia Officers, Removal of

Repealed.

Article 54. Staff and Non-commissioned Officers, by Whom Appointed

Repealed.

Article 55. Division of Militia into Brigades, Regiments, and companies

Repealed.

Article 56. Disbursements from Treasury

No moneys shall be issued out of the treasury of this state, and disposed of, (except such sums as may be appropriated for the redemption of bills of credit, or treasurer´s notes, or for the payment of interest arising thereon) but by warrant under the hand of the governor for the time being, by and with the advice and consent of the council, for the necessary support and defense of this state, and for the necessary protection and preservation of the inhabitants thereof, agreeably to the acts and resolves of the general court.

Article 57. Accounts of Military Stores

Repealed.

Article 58. Compensation of Governor and Council

The governor and council shall be compensated for their services, from time to time, by such grants as the general courts shall think reasonable.

Article 59. Salaries of Judges

Permanent and honorable salaries shall be established by law, for the justices of the superior court.

Council

Article 60. Councilors; Mode of Election, etc

There shall be biennially elected, by ballot, five councilors, for advising the governor in the executive part of government. The freeholders and other inhabitants in each county, qualified to vote for senators, shall some time in the month of November, give in their votes for one councilor; which votes shall be received, sorted, counted, certified, and returned to the secretary's office, in the same manner as the votes for senators, to be by the secretary laid before the senate and house of representatives on the first Wednesday following the first Tuesday of January.

Article 61. Vacancies, How Filled, if No Choice

and the person having a plurality of votes in any county, shall be considered as duly elected a councilor: But if no person shall have a plurality of votes in any county, the senate and house of representatives shall take the names of the two persons who have the highest number of votes in each county, and not elected, and out of those two shall elect by joint ballot, the councilor wanted for such county, and the qualifications for councilors shall be the same as for senator.

Article 62. Subsequent Vacancies; Governor to Convene; Duties

If any person thus chosen a councilor, shall be elected governor or member of either branch of the legislature, and shall accept the trust; or if any person elected a councilor, shall refuse to accept the office, or in case of the death, resignation, or removal of any councilor out of the state, the governor may issue a precept for the election of a new councilor in that county where such vacancy shall happen and the choice shall be in the same manner as before directed. and the governor shall have full power and authority to convene the council, from time to time, at his discretion; and, with them, or the majority of them, may and shall, from time to time hold a council, for ordering and directing the affairs of the state, according to the laws of the land.

Article 63. Impeachment of Councilors

The members of the council may be impeached by the house, and tried by the senate for bribery, corruption, malpractice, or maladministration.

Article 64. Secretary to Record Proceedings of Council

The resolutions and advice of the council shall be recorded by the secretary, in a register, and signed by all members present agreeing thereto; and this record may be called for at any time, by either house of the legislature; and any member of the council may enter his opinion contrary to the resolutions of the majority, with the reasons for such opinion.

Article 65. Councilor Districts Provided for

The legislature may, if the public good shall hereafter require it, divide the state into five districts, as nearly equal as may be, governing themselves by the number of population, each district to elect a councilor: and, in case of such division, the manner of the choice shall be conformable to the present mode of election in counties.

Article 66. Elections by Legislature May be Adjourned From Day to Day; Order Thereof

and, whereas the elections, appointed to be made by this constitution on the first Wednesday of January biennially, by the two houses of the legislature, may not be completed on that day, the said elections may be adjourned from day to day, until the same be completed; and the order of the elections shall be as follows - the vacancies in the senate, if any, shall be first filled up: The governor shall then be elected, provided there shall be no choice of him by the people: and afterwards, the two houses shall proceed to fill up the vacancy, if any, in the council.

Secretary, Treasurer, Etc.

Article 67. Election of Secretary and Treasurer

The secretary and treasurer shall be chosen by joint ballot of the senators and representatives assembled in one room.

Article 68. State Records, Where Kept; Duty of Secretary

The records of the state shall be kept in the office of the secretary, and he shall attend the governor and council, the senate and representatives, in person, or by deputy, as they may require.

Article 69. Deputy Secretary

The secretary of the state shall, at all times, have a deputy, to be by him appointed; for whose conduct in office he shall be responsible: and, in case of the death, removal, or inability of the secretary, his deputy shall exercise all the duties of the office of secretary of this state, until another shall be appointed.

Article 70. Secretary to Give Bond

The secretary, before he enters upon the business of his office, shall give bond, with sufficient sureties, in a reasonable sum, for the use of the state, for the punctual performance of his trust.

County Treasurer, Etc.

Article 71. County Treasurers, Registers of Probate, County Attorneys, Sheriffs, and Registers of Deeds Elected

The county treasurers, registers of probate, county attorneys, sheriffs and registers of deeds, shall be elected by the inhabitants of the several towns, in the several counties in the state, according to the method now practiced, and the laws of the state, Provided nevertheless the legislature shall have authority to alter the manner of certifying the votes, and the mode of electing those officers; but not so as to deprive the people of the right they now have of electing them.

Article 72. Counties May be Divided into Districts for Registering Deeds

and the legislature, on the application of the major part of the inhabitants of any county, shall have authority to divide the same into two districts for registering deeds, if to them it shall appear necessary; each district to elect a register of deeds: and before they enter upon the business of their offices, shall be respectively sworn faithfully to discharge the duties thereof, and shall severally give bond, with sufficient sureties, in a reasonable sum, for the use of the county for the punctual performance of their respective trusts.

Judiciary Power

Article 72-a. Supreme and Superior Courts

The judicial power of the state shall be vested in the supreme court, a trial court of general jurisdiction known as the superior court, and such lower courts as the legislature may establish under Article 4th of Part 2.

Article 73. Tenure of Office to be Expressed in Commissions; Judges to Hold Office During Good Behavior, etc.; Removal

The tenure that all commissioned officers shall have by law in their offices shall be expressed in their respective commissions, and all judicial officers duly appointed, commissioned and sworn, shall hold their offices during good behavior except those for whom a different provision is made in this constitution. The governor with consent of the council may remove any commissioned officer for reasonable cause upon the address of both houses of the legislature, provided nevertheless that the cause for removal shall be stated fully and substantially in the address and shall not be a cause which is a sufficient ground for impeachment, and provided further that no officer shall be so removed unless he shall have had an opportunity to be heard in his defense by a joint committee of both houses of the legislature.

Article 73-a. Supreme Court, Administration

The chief justice of the supreme court shall be the administrative head of all the courts. He shall, with the concurrence of a majority of the supreme court justices, make rules governing the administration of all courts in the state and the practice and procedure to be followed in all such courts. The rules so promulgated shall have the force and effect of law.

Article 74. Judges to Give Opinions, When

Each branch of the legislature as well as the governor and council shall have authority to require the opinions of the justices of the supreme court upon important questions of law and upon solemn occasions.

Article 75. Justices of Peace Commissioned for Five Years

in order that the people may not suffer from the long continuance in place of any justice of the peace who shall fail in discharging the important duties of his office with ability and fidelity, all commissions of justice of the peace shall become void at the expiration of five years from their respective dates, and upon the expiration of any commission, the same may if necessary be renewed or another person appointed as shall most conduce to the well being of the state.

Article 76 Divorce and Probate Appeals, Where Tried

All causes of marriage, divorce and alimony; and all appeals from the respective judges of probate shall be heard and tried by the superior court until the legislature shall by law make other provision.

Article 77. Jurisdiction of Justices in Civil Causes

The general court are empowered to give to justices of the peace jurisdiction in civil causes, when the damages demanded shall not exceed one hundred dollars and title of real estate is not concerned; but with right of appeal, to either party, to some other court. and the general court are further empowered to give to police courts original jurisdiction to try and determine, subject to right of appeal and trial by jury, all criminal causes wherein the punishment is less than imprisonment in the state prison.

Article 78. Judges and Sheriffs, When Disqualified by Age

No person shall hold the office of judge of any court, or judge of probate, or sheriff of any county, after he has attained the age of seventy years.

Article 79. Judges and Justices not to Act as Counsel

No judge of any court, or justice of the peace, shall act as attorney, or be of counsel, to any party, or originate any civil suit, in matters which shall come or be brought before him as judge, or justice of the peace.

Article 80. Jurisdiction and Term of Probate Courts

All matters relating to the probate of wills, and granting letters of administration, shall be exercised by the judges of probate, in such manner as the legislature have directed, or may hereafter direct: and the judges of probate shall hold their courts at such place or places, on such fixed days, as the conveniency of the people may require; and the legislature from time to time appoint.

Article 81. Judges and Registers of Probate not to Act as Counsel

No judge, or register of probate, shall be of counsel, act as advocate, or receive any fees as advocate or counsel, in any probate business which is pending, or may be brought into any court of probate in the county of which he is judge or register.

Clerk of the Courts

Article 82. Clerks of Courts, by Whom Appointed

The judges of the courts (those of probate excepted) shall appoint their respective clerks to hold their office during pleasure: and no such clerk shall act as an attorney or be of counsel in any cause in the court of which he is clerk, nor shall he draw any writ originating a civil action.

Encouragement of Literature, Trades, Etc.

Article 83. Encouragement of Literature, etc.; Control of Corporations, Monopolies, etc

Knowledge and learning, generally diffused through a community, being essential to the preservation of a free government; and spreading the opportunities and advantages of education through the various parts of the country, being highly conducive to promote this end; it shall be the duty of the legislators and magistrates, in all future periods of this government, to cherish the interest of literature and the sciences, and all seminaries and public schools, to encourage private and public institutions, rewards, and immunities for the promotion of agriculture, arts, sciences, commerce, trades, manufactures, and natural history of the country; to countenance and inculcate the principles of humanity and general benevolence, public and private charity, industry and economy, honesty and punctuality, sincerity, sobriety, and all social affections, and generous sentiments, among the people: Provided, nevertheless, that no money raised by taxation shall ever be granted or applied for the use of the schools of institutions of any religious sect or denomination. Free and fair competition in the trades and industries is an inherent and essential right of t he people and should be protected against all monopolies and conspiracies which tend to hinder or destroy it. The size and functions of all corporations should be so limited and regulated as to prohibit fictitious capitalization and provision should be made for the supervision and government thereof. Therefore, all just power possessed by the state is hereby granted to the general court to enact laws to prevent the operations within the state of all persons and associations, and all trusts and corporations, foreign or domestic, and the officers thereof, who endeavor to raise the price of any article of commerce or to destroy free and fair competition in the trades and industries through combination, conspiracy, monopoly, or any other unfair means; to control and regulate the acts of all such persons, associations, corporations, trusts, and officials doing business within the state; to prevent fictitious capitalization; and to authorize civil and criminal proceedings in respect to all the wrongs herein declared against.

Oaths and Subscriptions

Article 84. Oath of Civil Officers

Any person chosen governor, councilor, senator, or representative, military or civil officer, (town officers excepted) accepting the trust, shall, before he proceeds to execute the duties of his office, make and subscribe the following declaration, viz. -

I, A.B. do solemnly swear, that I will bear faith and true allegiance to the United States of America and the state of New Hampshire, and will support the constitution thereof. So help me God.

I, A.B. do solemnly and sincerely swear and affirm that I will faithfully and impartially discharge and perform all duties incumbent on me as ...., according to the best of my abilities, agreeably to the rules and regulations of this constitution and laws of the state of New Hampshire. So help me God.

Any person having taken and subscribed the oath of allegiance, and the same being filed in the secretary's office, he shall not be obliged to take said oath again.

Provided always, when any person chosen or appointed as aforesaid shall be of the denomination called Quakers, or shall be scrupulous of swearing, and shall decline taking the said oaths, such person shall take and subscribe them, omitting the word "swear," and likewise the words "So help me God," subjoining instead thereof, "This I do under the pains and penalties of perjury."

I, A.B., do solemnly and sincerely swear and affirm, that I will faithfully and impartially discharge and perform all the duties incumbent on me as....................according to the best of my abilities, agreeably to the rules and regulations of this constitution, and the laws of the State of New Hampshire. So help me God.

Article 85. Before Whom Taken

The oaths or affirmations shall be taken and subscribed by the governor before a justice of a New Hampshire court, in the presence of both houses of the legislature, by the senators and representatives before the governor and council for the time being, and by all other officers before such persons and in such manner as the general court shall from time to time appoint.

Article 86. Form of Commissions

All commissions shall be in the name of the state of New Hampshire, signed by the governor, and attested by the secretary, or his deputy, and shall have the great seal of the state affixed thereto.

Article 87. Form of Writs

All writs issuing out of the clerk's office in any of the courts of law, shall be in the name of the state of New Hampshire; shall be under the seal of the court whence they issue, and bear test of the chief, first, or senior justice of the court; but when such justice shall be interested, then the writ shall bear test of some other justice of the court, to which the same shall be returnable; and be signed by the clerk of such court.

Article 88. Form of Indictments, etc

All indictments, presentments, and informations, shall conclude,

"against the peace and dignity of the state."

Article 89. Suicides and Deodands

The estates of such persons as may destroy their own lives, shall not for that offense be forfeited, but descend or ascend in the same manner, as if such persons had died in a natural way. Nor shall any article, which shall accidentally occasion the death of any person, be henceforth deemed a deodand, or in any wise forfeited on account of such misfortune.

Article 90. Existing Laws Continued if not Repugnant

All the laws which have heretofore been adopted, used, and approved, in the province, colony, or state of New Hampshire, and usually practiced on in the courts of law, shall remain and be in full force, until altered and repealed by the legislature; such parts thereof only excepted, as are repugnant to the rights and liberties contained in this constitution: Provided that nothing herein contained, when compared with the twenty-third article in the bill of rights, shall be construed to affect the laws already made respecting the persons, or estates of absentees.

Article 91. Habeas Corpus

The privilege and benefit of the habeas corpus, shall be enjoyed in this state, in the most free, easy, cheap, expeditious, and ample manner, and shall not be suspended by the legislature, except upon most urgent and pressing occasions, and for a time not exceeding three months.

Article 92. Enacting Style of Statutes

The enacting style in making and passing acts, statutes, and laws, shall be, be it enacted by the Senate and House of Representatives in General Court convened.

Article 93. Governor and Judges Prohibited From Holding Other Offices

No governor, or judge of the supreme judicial court, shall hold any office or place under the authority of this state, except such as by this constitution they are admitted to hold, saving that the judges of the said court may hold the offices of justice of the peace throughout the state; nor shall they hold any place or office, or receive any pension or salary, from any other state, government, or power, whatever.

Article 94. Incompatibility of Offices; Only Two Offices of Profit to be Holden at Same Time

No person shall be capable of exercising, at the same time more than one of the following offices within this state, viz. judge of probate, sheriff, register of deeds; and never more than two offices of profit, which may be held by appointment of the governor, or governor and council, or senate and house of representatives, or superior or inferior courts; military offices, and offices of justice of the peace excepted.

Article 95. Incompatibility of Certain Offices

No person holding the office of judge of any court, (except special judges) secretary, treasurer of the state, attorney-general, register of deeds, sheriff, collectors of state and federal taxes, members of Congress or any person holding any office under the United States, including any person in active military service, shall at the same time hold the office of governor, or have a seat in the senate, or house of representatives, or council; but his being chosen and appointed to, and accepting the same, shall operate as a resignation of his seat in the chair, senate, or house of representatives, or council; and the place so vacated shall be filled up. No member of the council shall have a seat in the senate or house of representatives.

Article 96. Bribery and Corruption Disqualify for Office

No person shall ever be admitted to hold a seat in the legislature or any office of trust or importance under this government, who, in the due course of law, has been convicted of bribery or corruption, in obtaining an election or appointment.

Article 97. Value of Money, How Computed

Repealed.

Article 98. Constitution, When to Take Effect

to the end that there may be no failure of justice, or danger to the state, by the alterations and amendments made in the constitution, the general court is hereby fully authorized and directed to fix the time when the alterations and amendments shall take effect, and make the necessary arrangements accordingly.

Article 99. Revision of Constitution Provided For

Repealed.

Article 100. Alternate Methods of Proposing Amendments

Amendments to this constitution may be proposed by the general court or by a constitutional convention selected as herein provided.

(a) The senate and house of representatives, voting separately, may propose amendments by a three-fifths vote of the entire membership of each house at any session.

(b) The general court, by an affirmative vote of a majority of all members of both houses voting separately, may at any time submit the question "Shall there be a convention to amend or revise the constitution?" to the qualified voters of the state. If the question of holding a convention is not submitted to the people at some time during any period of ten years, it shall be submitted by the secretary of state at the general election in the tenth year following the last submission. If a majority of the qualified voters voting on the question of holding a convention approves it, delegates shall be chosen at the next regular general election, or at such earlier time as the legislature may provide, in the same manner and proportion as the representatives to the general court are chosen. The delegates so chosen shall convene at such time as the legislature may direct and may recess from time to time and make such rules for the conduct of their convention as they may determine.

(c) The constitutional convention may propose amendments by a three-fifths vote of the entire membership of the convention. Each constitutional amendment proposed by the general court or by a constitutional convention shall be submitted to the voters by written ballot at the next biennial November election and shall become a part of the Constitution only after approval by two-thirds of the qualified voters present and voting on the subject in the towns, wards, and unincorporated places.

Article 101. Enrollment of Constitution

This form of government shall be enrolled on parchment, and deposited in the secretary's office, and be a part of the laws of the land and printed copies thereof shall be prefixed to the books containing the laws of this state, in all future editions thereof.